Learn SAP Business One: A Comprehensive Guide for Beginners

Table of Contents:

C000161749

Chapter 1: Introduction to SAP Business One

Welcome to the first chapter of "Mastering SAP Business One: A Comprehensive Guide for Beginners." In this chapter, we will provide you with an introduction to SAP Business One, including its overview, key features, and benefits. By the end of this chapter, you will have a solid understanding of what SAP Business One is and how it can benefit your business.

Section 1: Overview of SAP Business One

SAP Business One is an integrated Enterprise Resource Planning (ERP) solution designed specifically for small and medium-sized enterprises (SMEs). It provides a comprehensive set of tools to manage various aspects of your business, such as finance, sales, purchasing, inventory, and production.

With SAP Business One, you can streamline your business processes, improve efficiency, gain better visibility into your operations, and make informed decisions based on real-time data. It offers a user-friendly interface and customizable features to adapt to your specific business needs.

Section 2: Key Features and Benefits

2.1 Scalability and Flexibility

SAP Business One is scalable, allowing you to start with the basic functionalities and gradually expand as your business grows. It can be easily tailored to your specific industry and business requirements, ensuring flexibility and adaptability.

2.2 Integrated Business Processes

One of the key advantages of SAP Business One is its integration capabilities. It provides a unified platform for managing various business functions, eliminating the need for separate software applications. This integration enables seamless data flow across departments, resulting in improved collaboration and efficiency.

2.3 Real-Time Analytics and Reporting

SAP Business One offers robust reporting and analytics capabilities. It allows you to generate real-time reports and dashboards, providing valuable insights into your business performance. With these analytical tools, you can monitor key metrics, identify trends, and make data-driven decisions to drive growth and profitability.

2.4 CRM and Sales Management

SAP Business One includes Customer Relationship Management (CRM) functionalities to help you manage your sales pipeline, track customer interactions, and improve customer satisfaction. It enables you to streamline your sales processes, automate tasks, and enhance customer engagement.

2.5 Inventory and Supply Chain Management

Efficiently managing inventory and the supply chain is crucial for any business. SAP Business One provides comprehensive inventory and supply chain management capabilities, including stock tracking, purchase order management, and demand planning. These features help optimize inventory levels, reduce costs, and ensure timely delivery to customers.

Section 3: Understanding the Target Audience

SAP Business One is specifically designed for small and medium-sized enterprises (SMEs) across various industries. It caters to businesses that require a comprehensive yet affordable ERP solution to manage their operations effectively. Whether you are in manufacturing, wholesale and distribution, retail, or service industry, SAP Business One can be tailored to meet your specific business needs.

This book is aimed at beginners who are new to SAP Business One and want to acquire a solid foundation in using the software. It assumes no prior knowledge of SAP Business One or ERP systems. Even if you have some familiarity with the software, this book will provide you with a systematic and comprehensive understanding of its features and functionalities.

In the next chapter, we will guide you through the process of installing SAP Business One and getting started with the software. So, let's dive in and embark on this exciting journey to master SAP Business One!

Section 4: Getting Started with SAP Business One

4.1 Installing SAP Business One

To begin your SAP Business One journey, you need to install the software on your system. Here are the steps to install SAP Business One:

Step 1: Obtain the Installation Files

Contact your SAP representative or visit the SAP website to obtain the installation files for SAP Business One. Make sure you have the correct version and any necessary license keys.

Step 2: System Requirements

Before installing, ensure that your system meets the minimum requirements specified by SAP. These requirements include hardware specifications, operating system compatibility, and database requirements.

Step 3: Run the Installation Wizard

Launch the installation wizard and follow the on-screen instructions. Select the desired installation type (server, client, or both) and provide the necessary information such as installation path and database details.

Step 4: Configure the Database

During the installation process, you will be prompted to configure the database. SAP Business One supports various databases such as Microsoft SQL Server and SAP HANA. Choose the appropriate database and provide the required credentials.

Step 5: Complete the Installation

Once the installation is complete, verify the installation by launching the SAP Business One client. Log in using the default credentials and ensure that you can access the system without any issues.

4.2 Navigating the User Interface

After successful installation, it's time to familiarize yourself with the SAP Business One user interface (UI). The UI consists of various elements that allow you to navigate and interact with the system effectively. Here are the key components:

Menu Bar: Located at the top of the screen, the menu bar provides access to different modules and functions within SAP Business One. It contains menus such as Sales, Purchasing, Inventory, and Financials.

Toolbars: Depending on the active window or module, you will find different toolbars that contain frequently used functions and shortcuts. These toolbars help you perform common tasks quickly.

Navigation Pane: The navigation pane is typically located on the left side of the screen and provides a hierarchical view of the modules, sub-modules, and their corresponding functions. Use the navigation pane to navigate to different areas of the system.

Workspaces: Workspaces allow you to customize the layout of SAP Business One according to your preferences. You can create multiple workspaces and arrange windows, reports, and dashboards to suit your workflow.

Data Entry Forms: Data entry forms are used to input and edit information in SAP Business One. They contain fields, checkboxes, dropdown lists, and other controls for entering data. Learn to navigate and fill in the required fields in these forms.

4.3 Setting Up User Preferences

Personalizing your user preferences in SAP Business One enhances your user experience. Here are some key preferences you can configure:

Language and Display Settings: Set your preferred language and customize the display settings such as font size and color scheme.

Date and Time Format: Configure the date and time format that aligns with your regional preferences.

System Alerts and Notifications: Specify the types of system alerts and notifications you want to receive, such as email notifications for pending approvals or critical issues.

Keyboard Shortcuts: Familiarize yourself with the available keyboard shortcuts to perform actions quickly, such as copying and pasting data or navigating between fields.

By configuring your user preferences, you can tailor SAP Business One to your liking and optimize your productivity within the system.

Congratulations! You have successfully installed SAP Business One and learned how to navigate its user interface and configure user preferences. In the next chapter, we will delve into the process of setting up your company and performing basic configuration in SAP Business One. Stay tuned!

Chapter 2: Basic Configuration and Setup

Section 1: Company Setup and Configuration

1.1 Creating a New Company

To start using SAP Business One, you need to set up your company in the system. Follow these steps to create a new company:

Step 1: Open SAP Business One

Launch SAP Business One and log in using your credentials.

Step 2: Access the Administration Module

Click on the "Administration" menu in the menu bar and select "Company Setup" from the dropdown menu.

Step 3: Create a New Company

In the Company Setup window, click on the "Add" button to create a new company. Fill in the required information such as company name, address, and contact details.

Step 4: Define Company Details

Provide additional details such as the company's default currency, fiscal year, and tax settings. You can also set up defaults for shipping and payment methods.

Step 5: Save the Company Configuration

Once you have entered all the necessary information, click "OK" to save the company configuration. SAP Business One will create a new database for your company.

1.2 Defining Business Partner Master Data

Business partners are entities such as customers, vendors, and leads that interact with your company. It is important to set up and maintain accurate business partner master data. Here's how:

Step 1: Access Business Partner Master Data

Navigate to the "Business Partners" menu in the menu bar and select "Business Partner Master Data" from the dropdown menu.

Step 2: Create a New Business Partner

Click on the "Add" button to create a new business partner. Select the appropriate business partner type (customer, vendor, or lead) and enter the relevant details such as name, address, contact information, and payment terms.

Step 3: Set Up Additional Information

Depending on the business partner type, you may need to provide additional information such as credit limits, tax IDs, and bank account details. Fill in the necessary fields accordingly.

Step 4: Save the Business Partner Data

After entering all the required information, click "OK" to save the business partner data. Repeat this process for each new business partner you need to set up.

Section 2: Configuring General Settings

2.1 Currencies and Exchange Rates

SAP Business One allows you to work with multiple currencies. Here's how to configure currencies and exchange rates:

Step 1: Access Currency Setup

Go to the "Administration" menu and select "Currency Setup" from the dropdown menu.

Step 2: Define Currencies

In the Currency Setup window, click on the "Add" button to define the currencies you want to use. Enter the currency code, description, and any relevant conversion factors.

Step 3: Set Up Exchange Rates

To define exchange rates, select "Exchange Rates" from the Currency Setup window. Enter the conversion rates between different currencies based on the prevailing market rates.

2.2 Tax Codes and Calculation Methods

Configuring tax codes and calculation methods is essential for accurate tax reporting and compliance. Follow these steps to set up tax-related settings:

Step 1: Access Tax Definition

In the "Administration" menu, select "Setup" and then choose "Tax" from the dropdown menu.

Step 2: Create Tax Codes

In the Tax Definition window, click on the "Add" button to create tax codes. Enter the tax code, description, tax type, and applicable tax rate.

Step 3: Define Tax Calculation Methods

To define tax calculation methods, select "Tax Calculation Methods" from the Tax Definition window. Set up calculation formulas based on your tax regulations and requirements.

Section 3: Creating Chart of Accounts and Financial Settings

3.1 Chart of Accounts

The chart of accounts is the foundation of your financial accounting system. Here's how to set it up:

Step 1: Access Chart of Accounts

In the "Administration" menu, select "Setup" and then choose "Financials" from the dropdown menu.

Step 2: Create Account Groups

Click on the "Account Groups" tab and define the account groups that align with your financial reporting needs.

Examples of account groups include assets, liabilities, revenues, and expenses.

Step 3: Define G/L Accounts

Switch to the "G/L Accounts" tab and create individual general ledger (G/L) accounts. Assign each account to the appropriate account group and provide the necessary details such as account code, description, and currency.

3.2 Financial Settings

Configuring financial settings ensures accurate recording and reporting of financial transactions. Follow these steps:

Step 1: Access Financial Setup

In the "Administration" menu, select "Setup" and then choose "Financials" from the dropdown menu.

Step 2: Define Posting Periods

Click on the "Posting Periods" tab and define the posting periods for your fiscal year. Set the start and end dates for each period, enabling proper control over transaction posting.

Step 3: Configure Opening Balances

Switch to the "Opening Balances" tab to enter the opening balances for your G/L accounts. Input the relevant account balances as of the starting date of your fiscal year.

Congratulations! You have completed the first chapter of "Mastering SAP Business One." In this chapter, we introduced you to SAP Business One, discussed its key features and benefits, and guided you through the process of installation, user interface navigation, and basic configuration and setup.

In the next chapter, we will dive deeper into master data management, covering topics such as item master data, business partner master data, and more. Stay tuned for an exciting journey into harnessing the power of SAP Business One!

Chapter 3: Master Data Management

Section 1: Managing Item Master Data

1.1 Creating Item Master Data

Item master data represents the products or services your company sells or purchases. Here's how to create item master data in SAP Business One:

Step 1: Access Item Master Data

Go to the "Inventory" menu in the menu bar and select "Item Master Data" from the dropdown menu.

Step 2: Create a New Item

Click on the "Add" button to create a new item. Enter the item code, description, and other relevant details such as pricing information, unit of measure, and item category.

Step 3: Specify Item Details

Provide additional information for the item, such as purchasing and sales data, tax settings, inventory information, and item properties. This data helps in managing and tracking the item accurately.

Step 4: Save the Item Master Data

Once you have entered all the necessary information, click "OK" to save the item master data. Repeat this process for each new item you need to create.

1.2 Item Pricing and Discounts

Setting up item pricing and discounts ensures accurate pricing calculations. Here's how to configure item pricing and discounts in SAP Business One:

Step 1: Access Item Pricing

In the "Inventory" menu, select "Price Lists" from the dropdown menu.

Step 2: Define Price Lists

Click on the "Add" button to create price lists for different customer groups or scenarios. Enter the price list name, currency, and any other relevant details.

Step 3: Set Item Prices

Within each price list, specify the prices for different items. You can define prices based on quantity breaks, date ranges, or customer-specific pricing.

Step 4: Apply Discounts

If you need to set up discounts, go to the "Discount Groups" section within the Price Lists window. Define discount groups and assign them to customers or customer groups. Specify the discount percentages or amounts for each group.

Section 2: Working with Business Partner Master Data

2.1 Creating Business Partner Master Data

Business partners, such as customers and vendors, play a crucial role in your business. Here's how to create business partner master data in SAP Business One:

Step 1: Access Business Partner Master Data

Go to the "Business Partners" menu in the menu bar and select "Business Partner Master Data" from the dropdown menu.

Step 2: Create a New Business Partner

Click on the "Add" button to create a new business partner. Select the appropriate business partner type (customer or vendor) and enter the relevant details such as name, address, contact information, and payment terms.

Step 3: Set Up Additional Information

Depending on the business partner type, you may need to provide additional information such as credit limits, tax IDs, and bank account details. Fill in the necessary fields accordingly.

Step 4: Save the Business Partner Data

After entering all the required information, click "OK" to save the business partner data. Repeat this process for each new business partner you need to create.

2.2 Managing Business Partner Activities

SAP Business One allows you to track and manage activities related to your business partners. Here's how to manage business partner activities:

Step 1: Access Business Partner Activities

In the "Business Partners" menu, select "Activities" from the dropdown menu.

Step 2: Create New Activities

Click on the "Add" button to create new activities such as phone calls, meetings, or tasks related to specific business partners. Enter the activity details, assign it to the appropriate business partner, and set a due date if necessary.

Step 3: Track Activity Status

Monitor the status of activities, update progress, and mark them as complete when finished. This helps ensure effective communication and follow-up with your business partners.

Section 3: Handling Banking Master Data

3.1 Managing Bank Master Data

Bank master data includes information about the banks your company works with. Here's how to manage bank master data in SAP Business One:

Step 1: Access Bank Master Data

In the "Banking" menu, select "Bank Master Data" from the dropdown menu.

Step 2: Create New Bank

Click on the "Add" button to create a new bank entry. Enter the bank name, address, and other relevant details.

Step 3: Set Up Bank Accounts

Within each bank entry, define the bank accounts associated with that bank. Specify the account number, currency, and other details as required.

Step 4: Save the Bank Master Data

After entering all the necessary information, click "OK" to save the bank master data. Repeat this process for each bank you work with.

3.2 Configuring Payment Methods

Payment methods define the ways your company receives and makes payments. Here's how to configure payment methods in SAP Business One:

Step 1: Access Payment Methods

In the "Banking" menu, select "Payment Methods" from the dropdown menu.

Step 2: Create New Payment Method

Click on the "Add" button to create a new payment method.
Enter the payment method name, description, and other
relevant details.

Step 3: Define Payment Parameters

Specify the parameters for the payment method, such as
default bank account, payment terms, and payment advice
information.

Step 4: Save the Payment Method Configuration

Once you have entered all the necessary information, click
"OK" to save the payment method configuration. Repeat this
process for each payment method you need to set up.

Congratulations! You have completed the second chapter of
"Mastering SAP Business One." In this chapter, we explored
master data management, focusing on item master data,
business partner master data, and banking master data.
These foundational elements are essential for running
various business processes effectively.

In the next chapter, we will delve into sales and distribution processes, guiding you through the creation of sales quotations, orders, deliveries, and more. Get ready to streamline your sales operations with SAP Business One!

Chapter 4: Sales and Distribution Processes

Section 1: Creating Sales Quotations

1.1 Accessing Sales Quotations

To begin the sales process, you can create sales quotations in SAP Business One. Follow these steps:

Step 1: Access Sales Quotations

Go to the "Sales" menu in the menu bar and select "Sales Quotation" from the dropdown menu.

Step 2: Create a New Sales Quotation

Click on the "Add" button to create a new sales quotation. Enter the relevant details such as customer, document date, and expiration date.

Step 3: Add Items to the Quotation

In the Items tab, add the items or services that the customer is interested in. Enter the quantity, unit price, and any other relevant details. You can also add additional text to provide more information about the quotation.

Step 4: Save the Sales Quotation

Once you have entered all the necessary information, click "OK" to save the sales quotation. You can then print or email the quotation to the customer for review.

1.2 Converting Sales Quotations to Sales Orders

After the customer accepts the quotation, you can convert it into a sales order. Here's how:

Step 1: Open the Sales Quotation

Locate the relevant sales quotation and open it in SAP Business One.

Step 2: Convert to Sales Order

In the sales quotation window, click on the "Copy to" button and select "Sales Order" from the dropdown menu.

Step 3: Verify and Adjust the Sales Order

Review the sales order details and make any necessary adjustments, such as updating quantities or adding additional items. Ensure that all the required information is accurate.

Step 4: Save the Sales Order

Once you have verified the sales order, click "OK" to save it. The sales order is now ready for further processing, such as delivery and invoicing.

Section 2: Managing Sales Orders and Deliveries

2.1 Processing Sales Orders

Once the sales order is created, you can manage and process it efficiently. Follow these steps:

Step 1: Access Sales Orders

Go to the "Sales" menu in the menu bar and select "Sales Order" from the dropdown menu.

Step 2: Locate the Sales Order

Locate the relevant sales order in the list or use the search function to find it.

Step 3: Review and Update the Sales Order

Open the sales order and review the details. Make any necessary changes, such as updating quantities or adding or removing items.

Step 4: Save and Process the Sales Order

Once you have made the necessary adjustments, click "OK" to save the changes. You can then proceed to process the sales order further, such as generating deliveries or invoices.

2.2 Generating Deliveries

Deliveries represent the fulfillment of sales orders by preparing and shipping the goods to customers. Here's how to generate deliveries in SAP Business One:

Step 1: Access Delivery

Go to the "Sales" menu in the menu bar and select "Delivery" from the dropdown menu.

Step 2: Create a New Delivery

Click on the "Add" button to create a new delivery. Select the sales order for which you want to generate the delivery.

Step 3: Add Items to the Delivery

In the Items tab, add the items that you are shipping to the customer. Enter the quantity, and SAP Business One will suggest the available stock for delivery.

Step 4: Save the Delivery

Once you have added all the relevant items, click "OK" to save the delivery. You can then print the delivery note and proceed with shipping the goods to the customer.

Section 3: Handling Sales Returns and Credit Memos

3.1 Processing Sales Returns

In cases where customers want to return items, you can process sales returns in SAP Business One. Follow these steps:

Step 1: Access Sales Returns

Go to the "Sales" menu in the menu bar and select "Sales Return" from the dropdown menu.

Step 2: Create a New Sales Return

Click on the "Add" button to create a new sales return. Select the customer and enter the relevant details such as the return date and reason for return.

Step 3: Add Returned Items

In the Items tab, add the items that the customer is returning. Enter the quantity and any other necessary details.

Step 4: Save the Sales Return

Once you have entered all the necessary information, click "OK" to save the sales return. You can then process the return further, such as generating a credit memo.

3.2 Generating Credit Memos

Credit memos are issued to customers to provide refunds or adjustments for returned items or other reasons. Here's how to generate credit memos in SAP Business One:

Step 1: Access Credit Memos

Go to the "Sales" menu in the menu bar and select "Credit Memo" from the dropdown menu.

Step 2: Create a New Credit Memo

Click on the "Add" button to create a new credit memo. Select the relevant customer and enter the necessary details such as the credit memo date and reason.

Step 3: Add Credit Memo Items

In the Items tab, add the items or charges for which you are issuing the credit memo. Enter the quantity, unit price, and any other relevant details.

Step 4: Save the Credit Memo

Once you have added all the necessary items, click "OK" to save the credit memo. You can then print or email the credit memo to the customer.

Congratulations! You have completed the fourth chapter of "Mastering SAP Business One." In this chapter, we explored the sales and distribution processes, including creating sales quotations, converting them to sales orders, generating deliveries, and handling sales returns and credit memos.

In the next chapter, we will dive into purchasing and procurement, guiding you through the creation of purchase orders, vendor management, goods receipts, and more. Get ready to streamline your procurement processes with SAP Business One!

Chapter 5: Purchasing and Procurement

Section 1: Creating Purchase Orders

1.1 Accessing Purchase Orders

To initiate the procurement process, you can create purchase orders in SAP Business One. Follow these steps:

Step 1: Access Purchase Orders

Go to the "Purchasing" menu in the menu bar and select "Purchase Order" from the dropdown menu.

Step 2: Create a New Purchase Order

Click on the "Add" button to create a new purchase order. Enter the relevant details such as the vendor, document date, and expected delivery date.

Step 3: Add Items to the Purchase Order

In the Items tab, add the items or services that you want to order from the vendor. Enter the quantity, unit price, and any other relevant details.

Step 4: Save the Purchase Order

Once you have entered all the necessary information, click "OK" to save the purchase order. You can then print or email the purchase order to the vendor for further processing.

1.2 Managing Purchase Requisitions

In some cases, you may need to create purchase requisitions to request goods or services internally before converting them into purchase orders. Here's how to manage purchase requisitions in SAP Business One:

Step 1: Access Purchase Requisitions

Go to the "Purchasing" menu in the menu bar and select "Purchase Requisition" from the dropdown menu.

Step 2: Create a New Purchase Requisition

Click on the "Add" button to create a new purchase requisition. Enter the relevant details such as the required date and the department responsible for the requisition.

Step 3: Add Items to the Purchase Requisition

In the Items tab, add the items or services that you need to request. Enter the quantity, unit price, and any other relevant details.

Step 4: Convert to Purchase Order

Once the purchase requisition is created, you can convert it into a purchase order by clicking the "Create PO" button. Review the details and save the purchase order accordingly.

Section 2: Vendor Management and Negotiations

2.1 Managing Vendor Master Data

Vendor master data contains information about your suppliers or service providers. Here's how to manage vendor master data in SAP Business One:

Step 1: Access Vendor Master Data

Go to the "Business Partners" menu in the menu bar and select "Business Partner Master Data" from the dropdown menu.

Step 2: Create a New Vendor

Click on the "Add" button to create a new vendor. Select the vendor type as "Vendor" and enter the relevant details such as the vendor's name, address, and contact information.

Step 3: Specify Vendor Details

Provide additional information for the vendor, such as payment terms, bank account details, tax information, and purchasing details.

Step 4: Save the Vendor Master Data

Once you have entered all the necessary information, click "OK" to save the vendor master data. Repeat this process for each new vendor you need to create.

2.2 Vendor Price Negotiations

Managing vendor price negotiations is crucial for achieving favorable procurement terms. Here's how to handle vendor price negotiations in SAP Business One:

Step 1: Access Purchase Quotations

Go to the "Purchasing" menu in the menu bar and select "Purchase Quotation" from the dropdown menu.

Step 2: Create a New Purchase Quotation

Click on the "Add" button to create a new purchase quotation. Select the relevant vendor and enter the necessary details such as the quotation date and expiration date.

Step 3: Add Items to the Quotation

In the Items tab, add the items or services for which you are requesting a quotation from the vendor. Enter the quantity, unit price, and any other relevant details.

Step 4: Save the Purchase Quotation

Once you have added all the necessary items, click "OK" to save the purchase quotation. You can then review the quotations received from vendors and negotiate prices accordingly.

Section 3: Receiving Goods and Managing Purchase Returns

3.1 Generating Goods Receipts

Goods receipts are created when you receive goods from your vendors. Here's how to generate goods receipts in SAP Business One:

Step 1: Access Goods Receipts

Go to the "Inventory" menu in the menu bar and select "Goods Receipt PO" from the dropdown menu.

Step 2: Create a New Goods Receipt

Click on the "Add" button to create a new goods receipt. Select the relevant purchase order for which you are receiving the goods.

Step 3: Add Received Items

In the Items tab, add the items that you have received from the vendor. Enter the quantity, and SAP Business One will update the inventory accordingly.

Step 4: Save the Goods Receipt

Once you have added all the received items, click "OK" to save the goods receipt. You can then print the goods receipt document and proceed with the necessary quality checks and stock updates.

3.2 Managing Purchase Returns

In case you need to return items to your vendors, you can process purchase returns in SAP Business One. Here's how:

Step 1: Access Purchase Returns

Go to the "Purchasing" menu in the menu bar and select "Purchase Return" from the dropdown menu.

Step 2: Create a New Purchase Return

Click on the "Add" button to create a new purchase return. Select the vendor and enter the necessary details such as the return date and reason for return.

Step 3: Add Return Items

In the Items tab, add the items that you are returning to the vendor. Enter the quantity and any other necessary details.

Step 4: Save the Purchase Return

Once you have entered all the necessary information, click "OK" to save the purchase return. You can then process the return further, such as generating a return document and initiating the return process with the vendor.

Congratulations! You have completed the fifth chapter of "Mastering SAP Business One." In this chapter, we explored purchasing and procurement processes, including creating purchase orders, managing vendor master data, generating goods receipts, and handling purchase returns.

In the next chapter, we will delve into inventory and warehouse management, guiding you through stock management, stock transfers, and warehouse operations. Get ready to optimize your inventory processes with SAP Business One!

Chapter 6: Inventory and Warehouse Management

Section 1: Stock Management

1.1 Managing Stock Levels

Effective stock management is crucial for maintaining optimal inventory levels. Here's how to manage stock levels in SAP Business One:

Step 1: Access Stock Management

Go to the "Inventory" menu in the menu bar and select "Item Master Data" from the dropdown menu.

Step 2: Review Stock Levels

Navigate to the "Stock Data" tab of the item master data. Here, you can view the current stock levels, including quantities on hand, committed quantities, and available quantities.

Step 3: Perform Stock Counting

To ensure accurate stock levels, conduct regular stock counts. Use the "Stock Counting" feature in SAP Business

One to record physical inventory counts and reconcile them with the system's records.

Step 4: Adjust Stock Levels

If discrepancies are found during stock counting, adjust the stock levels in SAP Business One to reflect the actual quantities. This can be done through stock adjustments or stock transfers, which we will explore further in the following sections.

1.2 Stock Valuation

Accurate stock valuation is essential for financial reporting. Here's how to manage stock valuation in SAP Business One:

Step 1: Access Stock Valuation

Go to the "Inventory" menu in the menu bar and select "Item Master Data" from the dropdown menu.

Step 2: Review Valuation Methods

Navigate to the "Accounting Data" tab of the item master data. Here, you can define the valuation method for each item, such as moving average or standard costing.

Step 3: Calculate Stock Valuation

SAP Business One automatically calculates the stock valuation based on the defined valuation method and the current stock levels. This valuation information is used for financial reporting and inventory analysis.

Section 2: Stock Transfers and Adjustments

2.1 Stock Transfers

Stock transfers allow you to move inventory between different locations or warehouses within your organization. Here's how to perform stock transfers in SAP Business One:

Step 1: Access Stock Transfers

Go to the "Inventory" menu in the menu bar and select "Stock Transfer" from the dropdown menu.

Step 2: Create a New Stock Transfer

Click on the "Add" button to create a new stock transfer. Select the source and destination warehouses, and enter the relevant details such as the transfer date.

Step 3: Add Items to the Stock Transfer

In the Items tab, add the items you want to transfer. Enter the quantity and any other necessary details.

Step 4: Save and Process the Stock Transfer

Once you have added all the items, click "OK" to save the stock transfer. You can then process the transfer, and the inventory will be updated accordingly in the source and destination warehouses.

2.2 Stock Adjustments

Stock adjustments are used to correct discrepancies between the physical stock and the system records. Here's how to perform stock adjustments in SAP Business One:

Step 1: Access Stock Adjustments

Go to the "Inventory" menu in the menu bar and select "Inventory Posting" from the dropdown menu.

Step 2: Create a New Stock Adjustment

Click on the "Add" button to create a new stock adjustment. Enter the relevant details such as the posting date and the warehouse where the adjustment is taking place.

Step 3: Adjust Stock Quantities

In the Items tab, select the items for which you want to adjust the quantities. Enter the adjusted quantities, taking into account any discrepancies found during stock counting.

Step 4: Save and Post the Stock Adjustment

Once you have made the necessary adjustments, click "OK" to save the stock adjustment. You can then post the adjustment, and the inventory quantities will be updated accordingly.

Section 3: Warehouse Operations

3.1 Warehouse Setup

Proper warehouse setup is essential for efficient warehouse operations. Here's how to configure warehouse settings in SAP Business One:

Step 1: Access Warehouse Setup

Go to the "Inventory" menu in the menu bar and select "Warehouse Setup" from the dropdown menu.

Step 2: Create Warehouses

Click on the "Add" button to create new warehouses. Enter the warehouse code, name, and other relevant details.

Step 3: Define Bin Locations

If your warehouses use bin locations for storage, define the bin locations within each warehouse. Specify the bin codes, descriptions, and capacity.

Step 4: Save the Warehouse Setup

Once you have entered all the necessary information, click "OK" to save the warehouse setup. Your warehouses are now ready for operations.

3.2 Warehouse Transfers

Warehouse transfers are used to move inventory between different bin locations within a warehouse. Here's how to perform warehouse transfers in SAP Business One:

Step 1: Access Warehouse Transfers

Go to the "Inventory" menu in the menu bar and select "Warehouse Transfer" from the dropdown menu.

Step 2: Create a New Warehouse Transfer

Click on the "Add" button to create a new warehouse transfer. Select the source and destination bin locations within the same warehouse.

Step 3: Add Items to the Warehouse Transfer

In the Items tab, add the items you want to transfer. Enter the quantity and any other necessary details.

Step 4: Save and Process the Warehouse Transfer

Once you have added all the items, click "OK" to save the warehouse transfer. You can then process the transfer, and the inventory will be updated accordingly in the source and destination bin locations.

Congratulations! You have completed the sixth chapter of "Mastering SAP Business One." In this chapter, we explored inventory and warehouse management, including stock management, stock transfers, adjustments, and warehouse operations.

In the next chapter, we will delve into financial management, covering topics such as financial accounting, banking, and reporting in SAP Business One. Get ready to gain insights into your business's financial performance with SAP Business One!

Chapter 7: Financial Management

Section 1: Financial Accounting

1.1 General Ledger

The General Ledger (G/L) is the core component of financial accounting in SAP Business One. Here's how to manage G/L accounts:

Step 1: Access Chart of Accounts

Go to the "Financials" menu in the menu bar and select "Chart of Accounts" from the dropdown menu.

Step 2: Manage G/L Accounts

In the Chart of Accounts window, you can view and manage the G/L accounts. Create new accounts, edit existing ones, and assign them to the appropriate account groups.

Step 3: Define Account Codes and Descriptions

Enter unique account codes and meaningful descriptions for each G/L account to accurately categorize and track financial transactions.

1.2 Journal Entries

Journal entries allow you to record financial transactions in SAP Business One. Here's how to create journal entries:

Step 1: Access Journal Entries

Go to the "Financials" menu in the menu bar and select "Journal Entry" from the dropdown menu.

Step 2: Create a New Journal Entry

Click on the "Add" button to create a new journal entry. Enter the relevant details such as the posting date and journal entry type.

Step 3: Enter Transaction Details

In the Lines tab, enter the transaction details, including the G/L accounts, debit or credit amounts, and any additional information or references.

Step 4: Save the Journal Entry

Once you have entered all the necessary information, click "OK" to save the journal entry. The financial transaction will be recorded in the G/L accounts.

Section 2: Banking and Payments

2.1 Bank Reconciliation

Bank reconciliation helps you match your bank statement with your SAP Business One records. Here's how to perform bank reconciliation:

Step 1: Access Bank Reconciliation

Go to the "Banking" menu in the menu bar and select "Bank Reconciliation" from the dropdown menu.

Step 2: Select Bank Account and Statement

Choose the bank account for reconciliation and import the bank statement file or enter the statement details manually.

Step 3: Match Transactions

Match the transactions listed in the bank statement with the corresponding transactions in SAP Business One. Mark them as cleared to reconcile the accounts.

Step 4: Complete the Reconciliation

Review the reconciliation summary and confirm the reconciliation. Any discrepancies or outstanding items should be investigated and resolved.

2.2 Payments and Receivables

Managing payments and receivables is essential for cash flow management. Here's how to handle payments and receivables in SAP Business One:

Step 1: Access Payment Management

Go to the "Banking" menu in the menu bar and select "Payment Management" from the dropdown menu.

Step 2: Process Incoming Payments

Enter incoming payment details received from customers, including the customer, invoice references, payment amount, and payment method.

Step 3: Manage Outgoing Payments

Record outgoing payments made to vendors or other parties by entering payment details, including the vendor, invoice references, payment amount, and payment method.

Step 4: Review and Reconcile Receivables

Regularly review and reconcile receivables to ensure accurate tracking of outstanding customer payments. Follow up with customers for overdue payments and take necessary actions.

Section 3: Financial Reporting

3.1 Financial Statements

SAP Business One provides various financial statements to analyze your company's financial performance. Here's how to generate financial statements:

Step 1: Access Financial Reports

Go to the "Financials" menu in the menu bar and select "Financial Reports" from the dropdown menu.

Step 2: Choose the Financial Statement

Select the desired financial statement, such as the Balance Sheet or Income Statement.

Step 3: Define Reporting Parameters

Specify the reporting period, currency, and any other required parameters for the financial statement.

Step 4: Generate and Analyze the Statement

Click "Generate" to create the financial statement. Analyze the data presented to gain insights into your company's financial performance.

3.2 Customized Reports

SAP Business One allows you to create custom reports to meet your specific reporting needs. Here's how to create customized reports:

Step 1: Access Report and Layout Manager

Go to the "Tools" menu in the menu bar and select "Report and Layout Manager" from the dropdown menu.

Step 2: Create a New Report

Click on the "Add" button to create a new report. Define the report parameters, including data sources, filters, and layout design.

Step 3: Design the Report Layout

Use the Report and Layout Manager tools to design the report layout, including adding fields, formatting, and calculations.

Step 4: Save and Run the Custom Report

Once you have designed the report, save it and run it whenever needed to generate the customized report based on your defined parameters.

Congratulations! You have completed the seventh chapter of "Mastering SAP Business One." In this chapter, we explored financial management, including financial accounting, banking and payments, and financial reporting.

In the next chapter, we will focus on business analytics and reporting, covering topics such as dashboards, analytics tools, and key performance indicators in SAP Business One. Get ready to gain valuable insights for data-driven decision-making with SAP Business One!

Chapter 8: Business Analytics and Reporting

Section 1: SAP Business One Dashboards

1.1 Accessing Dashboards

SAP Business One provides interactive dashboards for visualizing key business data. Here's how to access and utilize dashboards:

Step 1: Access Dashboards

Go to the "Business Partners" menu in the menu bar and select "Dashboards" from the dropdown menu.

Step 2: Choose a Dashboard Template

Select a pre-built dashboard template that aligns with the metrics and insights you want to monitor. Choose from options such as sales, inventory, financials, or custom dashboards.

Step 3: Customize Dashboard Content

Modify the dashboard by adding or removing widgets, charts, or KPIs to fit your specific reporting requirements. Configure the dashboard to display the relevant data sources and time periods.

Step 4: Analyze and Monitor Data

Once the dashboard is configured, review the visualized data, charts, and KPIs to gain valuable insights into various aspects of your business. Monitor key metrics and performance indicators in real-time.

Section 2: Analytics Tools in SAP Business One

2.1 Query Generator

The Query Generator in SAP Business One allows you to create custom queries to retrieve specific data from your database. Here's how to use the Query Generator:

Step 1: Access Query Generator

Go to the "Tools" menu in the menu bar and select "Query Generator" from the dropdown menu.

Step 2: Define Query Parameters

Specify the tables, fields, and conditions for your query. Choose the data sources and define the criteria to filter the results.

Step 3: Generate and Execute the Query

Click "Generate" to create the SQL query based on the defined parameters. Execute the query to retrieve the desired data from your SAP Business One database.

Step 4: Analyze and Export Query Results

Review the query results, which will be displayed in a table format. Analyze the data and export it to other formats, such as Excel or CSV, for further analysis or reporting.

2.2 Crystal Reports

Crystal Reports is a powerful reporting tool integrated with SAP Business One. Here's how to create customized reports using Crystal Reports:

Step 1: Access Crystal Reports

Go to the "Tools" menu in the menu bar and select "Crystal Reports" from the dropdown menu.

Step 2: Create a New Report

Click on the "New" button to create a new Crystal Report. Define the report parameters, including data sources, fields, and layout design.

Step 3: Design the Report Layout

Utilize the Crystal Reports design interface to design the report layout. Add fields, apply formatting, insert charts or graphs, and include calculations or summaries as needed.

Step 4: Preview and Distribute the Report

Preview the report to ensure it meets your requirements. Once satisfied, save and distribute the report to relevant stakeholders in various formats, such as PDF or Excel.

Section 3: Key Performance Indicators (KPIs)

3.1 Creating KPIs

Key Performance Indicators (KPIs) provide insights into the performance of specific business processes. Here's how to create KPIs in SAP Business One:

Step 1: Access KPIs

Go to the "Business Partners" menu in the menu bar and select "KPIs" from the dropdown menu.

Step 2: Define KPI Parameters

Specify the KPI details, including the source data, calculation method, target values, and time periods.

Step 3: Set Thresholds and Indicators

Determine the thresholds and indicators for your KPIs, such as green, yellow, and red zones based on performance levels.

Step 4: Monitor and Analyze KPIs

Once the KPIs are set up, monitor and analyze the performance indicators regularly. Use the KPIs to identify trends, areas for improvement, and make data-driven decisions.

Section 4: SAP Business One Analytics

4.1 SAP Analytics Cloud

SAP Business One integrates with SAP Analytics Cloud, a comprehensive analytics platform. Here's how to leverage SAP Analytics Cloud for advanced analytics:

Step 1: Access SAP Analytics Cloud

Integrate your SAP Business One data with SAP Analytics Cloud by connecting the systems and setting up data synchronization.

Step 2: Create Analytics Models

Build analytical models in SAP Analytics Cloud to combine data from multiple sources, define relationships, and perform advanced calculations.

Step 3: Design Visualizations and Dashboards

Utilize the intuitive interface of SAP Analytics Cloud to create interactive visualizations, dashboards, and reports based on your analytical models.

Step 4: Perform Advanced Analysis

Leverage advanced analytics capabilities in SAP Analytics Cloud, such as predictive modeling, machine learning, and "what-if" scenarios, to gain deeper insights into your business data.

Congratulations! You have completed the eighth chapter of "Mastering SAP Business One." In this chapter, we explored business analytics and reporting, including SAP Business One dashboards, analytics tools such as Query Generator and Crystal Reports, key performance indicators (KPIs), and integration with SAP Analytics Cloud.

In the final chapter, we will cover system administration and user management in SAP Business One, ensuring the smooth operation and security of your SAP Business One environment. Get ready to learn essential administration tasks and best practices!

Chapter 9: System Administration and User Management

Section 1: System Setup

1.1 Company Setup

Proper system setup is essential for the smooth operation of SAP Business One. Here's how to configure the company settings:

Step 1: Access Company Setup

Go to the "Administration" menu in the menu bar and select "System Initialization" from the dropdown menu. Then choose "Company Details" to access the company setup.

Step 2: Configure General Settings

Enter the company name, address, contact information, and other general details in the Company Details window. Set the default currency, working hours, and other relevant settings.

Step 3: Customize System Behavior

Navigate to the various tabs in the Company Details window to configure specific aspects such as financials, inventory, purchasing, sales, and production settings according to your business requirements.

Step 4: Save the Company Setup

Once you have completed the necessary configurations, click "OK" to save the company setup. Ensure to review and verify the settings periodically to keep them up to date.

1.2 User and Authorization Setup

User management and authorization control are crucial for maintaining system security. Here's how to set up users and authorizations:

Step 1: Access User and Authorization Management

Go to the "Administration" menu in the menu bar and select "System Initialization" from the dropdown menu. Then choose "User and Authorization Management" to access the user setup.

Step 2: Create User Accounts

Click on the "Add" button to create new user accounts. Enter the user details such as name, username, password, and contact information.

Step 3: Define User Authorizations

Assign appropriate authorization levels to each user account based on their roles and responsibilities. Define the modules, windows, and actions that each user can access or perform.

Step 4: Save User and Authorization Setup

Once you have assigned the authorizations, click "OK" to save the user and authorization setup. Regularly review and update user permissions as roles or responsibilities change within your organization.

Section 2: Backup and Restore

2.1 Backup Strategy

Regular data backups are essential for protecting your business-critical information. Here's how to set up a backup strategy for SAP Business One:

Step 1: Determine Backup Frequency

Assess your business requirements and data sensitivity to determine how often backups should be performed. Consider factors such as transaction volume and criticality of the data.

Step 2: Select Backup Method

Choose a suitable backup method, such as full backups or incremental backups, based on your data volume, storage capacity, and recovery time objectives.

Step 3: Configure Backup Parameters

Set up backup parameters within SAP Business One, including the backup location, retention periods, and any compression or encryption options.

Step 4: Test and Validate Backups

Regularly test and validate the backup files to ensure their integrity and accessibility. Perform trial restorations to verify that the backup data can be successfully restored when needed.

2.2 Restore Procedures

In the event of data loss or system failure, it's crucial to know how to restore your SAP Business One environment. Here's how to perform data restoration:

Step 1: Access Restore Functionality

Refer to your backup solution and follow the provided instructions to access the restore functionality.

Step 2: Select Backup Files

Choose the relevant backup files to restore based on the date, time, or backup sets. Ensure you have the necessary backup media or access to the backup location.

Step 3: Perform Data Restoration

Follow the steps provided by your backup solution to restore the backup files. Ensure that the restored data is properly validated and consistent with the backup version.

Step 4: Test Restored Data

After the restoration process, thoroughly test the restored data to confirm its accuracy and integrity. Validate the functionality and verify that all critical data is accessible.

Section 3: System Monitoring and Performance

3.1 Monitoring System Health

Regular monitoring of your SAP Business One system helps ensure optimal performance and identifies any potential issues. Here's how to monitor system health:

Step 1: Utilize System Monitoring Tools

Leverage the built-in monitoring tools provided by SAP Business One to monitor system health. These tools offer insights into system performance, resource utilization, and potential bottlenecks.

Step 2: Monitor System Logs

Regularly review the system logs to identify any errors, warnings, or critical events. Address any issues promptly to prevent system instability or data loss.

Step 3: Implement Proactive Maintenance

Perform routine system maintenance tasks, such as database cleanup, index optimization, and periodic system restarts, to maintain system performance and stability.

Step 4: Engage Support and Consult Resources

If you encounter any system issues or require assistance, engage SAP support or consult relevant resources, such as documentation, forums, or user groups, to troubleshoot and resolve the problems effectively.

3.2 Performance Optimization

Optimizing system performance ensures efficient operations and user satisfaction. Here are some tips for performance optimization:

Step 1: Analyze Performance Metrics

Utilize the performance monitoring tools to analyze key metrics, such as response times, database performance, and user activity, to identify performance bottlenecks.

Step 2: Identify Performance Improvement Opportunities

Based on the analysis, identify areas for improvement, such as query optimization, index tuning, hardware upgrades, or system configuration adjustments.

Step 3: Implement Performance Enhancements

Implement the recommended performance enhancements, following best practices and guidelines provided by SAP Business One. This may involve database optimizations, system tuning, or infrastructure enhancements.

Step 4: Monitor and Evaluate Performance

Continuously monitor the system performance after implementing the enhancements. Assess the impact and validate the effectiveness of the optimizations. Make further adjustments if necessary.

Congratulations! You have completed the ninth chapter of "Mastering SAP Business One." In this chapter, we explored system administration and user management, including system setup, user and authorization management, backup and restore procedures, and system monitoring and performance optimization.

By effectively managing the system administration tasks, you can ensure the smooth operation, security, and performance of your SAP Business One environment.

Chapter 10: Advanced Features and Integration

Section 1: Integration with Other Systems

1.1 Integration Options

SAP Business One offers various integration capabilities to connect with other systems and enhance business processes. Here are some integration options:

Step 1: Evaluate Integration Requirements

Assess your business needs and identify the systems or applications that require integration with SAP Business One. Determine the data flow, integration frequency, and desired outcomes.

Step 2: Explore Integration Tools

SAP Business One provides integration tools such as the Integration Framework, Data Transfer Workbench, or Web Services. Understand the capabilities and features of each tool to select the most suitable one for your integration needs.

Step 3: Configure Integration Settings

Follow the specific instructions and guidelines provided by the integration tool to configure the integration settings. This may involve mapping data fields, defining synchronization schedules, or establishing communication protocols.

Step 4: Test and Validate Integration

After configuring the integration, perform thorough testing to ensure that data is accurately transferred between systems. Validate the integration by verifying data consistency, synchronization, and any automation or workflow processes.

1.2 Examples of Integration Scenarios

SAP Business One can be integrated with various systems to streamline operations and enable seamless data exchange. Here are some common integration scenarios:

Integration with E-commerce Platforms: Integrate SAP Business One with your e-commerce platform to automate order processing, inventory synchronization, and customer data management.

CRM Integration: Connect SAP Business One with Customer Relationship Management (CRM) systems to synchronize customer data, sales activities, and customer interactions for enhanced customer management.

Third-Party Applications Integration: Integrate SAP Business One with third-party applications, such as payroll systems or human resources management systems, to streamline data exchange and eliminate manual data entry.

Business Intelligence Integration: Integrate SAP Business One with business intelligence tools or data analytics platforms to leverage advanced reporting and analytics capabilities for in-depth business insights.

Section 2: Advanced Functionality

2.1 Production Management

SAP Business One offers production management capabilities to streamline manufacturing processes. Here's how to utilize production management features:

Step 1: Set Up Production Parameters

Configure production-related parameters, such as Bill of Materials (BOM), routing, work centers, and production stages, to define the manufacturing process.

Step 2: Create Production Orders

Generate production orders to initiate the manufacturing process. Define the order quantity, materials required, and schedule for production.

Step 3: Monitor Production Progress

Track the progress of production orders, including work in progress, material consumption, and labor utilization. Update the production order status as each manufacturing stage is completed.

Step 4: Perform Goods Receipt and Production Costing

Upon completion of production, perform a goods receipt to receive the finished goods into inventory. Calculate production costs and update relevant financial records for accurate costing and inventory valuation.

2.2 Service Management

SAP Business One includes service management features to effectively manage service-related activities. Here's how to utilize service management capabilities:

Step 1: Create Service Calls

Create service calls to record customer requests or issues. Capture details such as the customer, contact information, problem description, and priority level.

Step 2: Assign and Dispatch Service Technicians

Assign service technicians to the service calls based on their skills, availability, and geographic location. Dispatch technicians to the customer site to resolve the service issues.

Step 3: Track Service Activities

Monitor and track service activities, including service status, response times, resolution times, and materials utilized. Update the service call with relevant information and maintain a complete service history.

Step 4: Perform Service Billing

Generate service invoices based on the services provided and any associated charges. Link service calls to invoices for accurate billing and revenue recognition.

Section 3: Customization and Extensions

3.1 Customization Options

SAP Business One allows for customization to adapt the system to your specific business requirements. Here are some customization options:

Step 1: Identify Customization Needs

Determine the specific areas of SAP Business One that require customization to meet your business processes or unique industry requirements.

Step 2: Utilize User-Defined Fields and Tables

Leverage user-defined fields and tables within SAP Business One to capture additional data or create custom data structures to accommodate specific information.

Step 3: Enhance Functionality with Add-Ons

Explore available add-ons or extensions developed by SAP partners or third-party vendors to extend the functionality of SAP Business One. These add-ons can provide specialized features for specific industries or business needs.

Step 4: Work with SAP Partners or Developers

Engage SAP partners or developers to create customizations or develop tailored solutions to address your unique business requirements. Collaborate with them to design, develop, and implement the desired customizations or extensions.

3.2 Upgrade Considerations

When upgrading SAP Business One, it's essential to consider the impact on customizations and extensions. Here are some key considerations:

Step 1: Assess Compatibility with New Versions

Verify the compatibility of your customizations or extensions with the new version of SAP Business One. Determine if any modifications or updates are required to ensure seamless operation after the upgrade.

Step 2: Test Customizations and Extensions

Perform thorough testing of your customizations or extensions in the upgraded SAP Business One environment. Validate their functionality, data integrity, and compatibility with other system components.

Step 3: Engage SAP Partners or Developers

Collaborate with SAP partners or developers to address any compatibility issues or upgrade-related challenges. Seek their guidance and support to update or adapt your customizations or extensions to the new version.

Step 4: Plan for Training and User Adoption

Ensure that users are trained on any changes resulting from the upgrade, including updates to customizations or extensions. Provide necessary documentation and support to facilitate a smooth transition and user adoption.

Congratulations! You have completed the tenth chapter of "Mastering SAP Business One." In this chapter, we explored advanced features and integration options, including integrating with other systems, utilizing advanced functionality such as production management and service management, and customization and extension possibilities.

By harnessing these advanced features and integrating SAP Business One with other systems, you can optimize your business processes and tailor the system to meet your specific needs.

Chapter 11: Best Practices and Tips

Section 1: Best Practices for SAP Business One Implementation

1.1 Define Clear Objectives

Before implementing SAP Business One, define clear objectives and goals for the project. Identify the specific business processes and areas that need improvement or automation.

1.2 Engage Stakeholders

Involve key stakeholders from different departments and levels of the organization in the implementation process. Their insights and feedback will contribute to a successful implementation.

1.3 Plan and Prepare Data Migration

Ensure proper planning and preparation for data migration from existing systems to SAP Business One. Cleanse and validate data to ensure accuracy and integrity during the migration process.

1.4 Conduct User Training

Provide comprehensive training to users on SAP Business One functionalities and processes. Empower them to effectively utilize the system and maximize its benefits.

1.5 Perform System Testing

Conduct thorough testing of SAP Business One before going live. Test various scenarios, processes, and integrations to identify and resolve any issues or gaps.

Section 2: Tips for Efficient System Usage

2.1 Regular System Maintenance

Perform regular system maintenance tasks, such as database backups, system updates, and optimization activities. This ensures the system's performance, stability, and security.

2.2 Document Processes and Procedures

Document your business processes and procedures within SAP Business One. This documentation serves as a reference and aids in training new users or troubleshooting issues.

2.3 Utilize Reporting and Analytics

Leverage the reporting and analytics capabilities of SAP Business One to gain insights into your business performance. Regularly review and analyze reports to make informed decisions.

2.4 Stay Informed about Updates and Enhancements

Stay updated with the latest SAP Business One releases, updates, and enhancements. This knowledge allows you to take advantage of new features and improvements that can benefit your business.

Section 3: Enhancing User Experience

3.1 Customize User Interface

Tailor the SAP Business One user interface to match the specific needs and preferences of your users. Customize menus, screen layouts, and shortcuts to improve usability and efficiency.

3.2 Enable Mobile Access

Leverage mobile access capabilities of SAP Business One to provide users with remote access to critical information and functionalities. This enables greater flexibility and productivity.

3.3 Encourage User Feedback

Create a culture of feedback and continuous improvement by actively seeking input from users. Encourage them to provide suggestions and insights to enhance the system and user experience.

3.4 Foster Collaboration and Knowledge Sharing

Promote collaboration among SAP Business One users by facilitating knowledge sharing and best practice sharing. Encourage users to learn from each other and collaborate on process improvements.

Congratulations! You have completed the eleventh chapter of "Mastering SAP Business One." In this chapter, we explored best practices for SAP Business One implementation, tips for efficient system usage, and strategies to enhance user experience.

By following these best practices, utilizing efficient system usage tips, and enhancing the user experience, you can maximize the benefits of SAP Business One and drive business growth and success.

Chapter 12: Troubleshooting and Support

Section 1: Troubleshooting Common Issues

1.1 System Performance Issues

Check system resources such as memory, CPU, and disk usage.

Optimize database performance by performing regular maintenance tasks such as reindexing and database cleanup.

Analyze system logs for errors or warnings and address any identified issues.

Review customizations or add-ons that may impact system performance and make necessary adjustments.

1.2 Integration Problems

Verify the integration setup and configurations, including data mappings and communication protocols.

Test connectivity between systems and troubleshoot any network or firewall issues.

Ensure that the integrated systems are using compatible versions and updates.

Check for error messages or logs related to the integration and investigate accordingly.

1.3 Data Inconsistencies

Review data entry processes and verify if proper validations and controls are in place.

Perform data integrity checks and compare data between relevant modules or reports.

Check for any system customization or extensions that may affect data consistency.

Analyze error messages or logs related to data inconsistencies and take corrective actions.

Section 2: Seeking Support

2.1 SAP Support Portal

Access the SAP Support Portal for comprehensive documentation, knowledge base articles, and user forums.

Search for solutions to common issues and troubleshooting guides.

Submit support tickets for assistance from SAP support experts.

2.2 Community and User Groups

Engage with the SAP Business One community through online forums and user groups.

Share your experiences, ask questions, and learn from other users' insights.

Seek advice and best practices from experienced users and consultants.

2.3 SAP Partners and Consultants

Collaborate with SAP partners or consultants for specialized support, implementation guidance, or customized solutions.

Engage their expertise for troubleshooting complex issues or optimizing system performance.

Leverage their knowledge of industry-specific requirements and best practices.

Section 3: Continuous Learning and Improvement

3.1 SAP Learning Hub

Access the SAP Learning Hub for self-paced e-learning courses, training materials, and certifications.

Stay updated with the latest SAP Business One functionalities, updates, and best practices.

3.2 User Training and Education

Invest in ongoing user training and education to enhance user proficiency and system utilization.

Conduct regular training sessions or workshops to address new features or processes.

3.3 System Documentation and Knowledge Base

Maintain comprehensive documentation of your system setup, configurations, and customizations.

Create an internal knowledge base with troubleshooting guides, FAQs, and best practice documents.

3.4 Periodic System Health Checks

Perform periodic system health checks to identify and address potential issues before they escalate.

Review system logs, conduct performance analyses, and validate data consistency.

Congratulations! You have completed the twelfth chapter of "Mastering SAP Business One." In this chapter, we explored troubleshooting common issues that may arise in SAP Business One, seeking support through various channels, and the importance of continuous learning and improvement.

By effectively troubleshooting issues, seeking the right support, and continuously learning and improving, you can ensure the smooth operation and optimal utilization of SAP Business One in your organization.

Chapter 13: Future Trends and Innovations in SAP Business One

Section 1: Cloud Technology

1.1 Cloud Deployment

Explore the benefits of cloud deployment for SAP Business One, such as scalability, flexibility, and reduced infrastructure costs.

Evaluate options for cloud hosting, whether through public cloud providers, private cloud environments, or hybrid cloud solutions.

1.2 Software as a Service (SaaS)

Consider the adoption of SAP Business One as a SaaS offering, where the software is delivered over the internet on a subscription basis.

Assess the advantages of SaaS, including easy access, automatic updates, and simplified management.

Section 2: Artificial Intelligence and Machine Learning

2.1 Intelligent Automation

Discover how AI and machine learning can be leveraged in SAP Business One to automate repetitive tasks, improve accuracy, and enhance decision-making processes.

Explore features such as automated data entry, intelligent document processing, or predictive analytics.

2.2 Chatbots and Virtual Assistants

Learn about the integration of chatbots and virtual assistants within SAP Business One to provide user support, answer inquiries, and perform routine tasks.

Evaluate the benefits of natural language processing and conversational interfaces for user engagement and productivity.

Section 3: Internet of Things (IoT) Integration

3.1 IoT Sensor Integration

Understand how IoT sensors can be integrated with SAP Business One to capture real-time data from connected devices or equipment.

Explore use cases such as asset tracking, predictive maintenance, or supply chain optimization.

3.2 Data Analytics and Insights

Utilize the data collected from IoT devices to gain valuable insights through advanced analytics and reporting capabilities within SAP Business One.

Leverage IoT data to optimize operations, identify patterns, and make data-driven decisions.

Section 4: Enhanced Mobility and User Experience

4.1 Mobile Applications

Embrace the use of mobile applications that allow users to access SAP Business One functionalities and data on their smartphones or tablets.

Enable remote access, real-time notifications, and on-the-go approvals for enhanced productivity.

4.2 User Interface Enhancements

Stay updated with user interface enhancements and improvements in SAP Business One, such as modernized design, intuitive navigation, and personalized dashboards.

Customize the user interface to align with the specific needs and preferences of your users.

Section 5: Advanced Analytics and Reporting

5.1 Embedded Analytics

Explore the integration of advanced analytics tools and capabilities within SAP Business One for in-depth data analysis and visualization.

Gain insights into sales trends, customer behavior, inventory optimization, or financial forecasting.

5.2 Predictive Analytics

Leverage predictive analytics algorithms and models to forecast trends, identify risks, and optimize business outcomes.

Apply predictive analytics to areas such as demand forecasting, sales forecasting, or customer churn analysis.

Congratulations! You have completed the thirteenth chapter of "Mastering SAP Business One." In this chapter, we explored future trends and innovations in SAP Business One, including cloud technology, artificial intelligence and machine learning, IoT integration, enhanced mobility and user experience, and advanced analytics and reporting.

By staying informed about these trends and innovations, you can position your organization to take advantage of emerging technologies and drive business growth and efficiency with SAP Business One.

Chapter 14: Conclusion and Final Thoughts

Congratulations! You have completed "Mastering SAP Business One." Throughout this book, we have covered a wide range of topics, starting from the basics of SAP Business One and gradually delving into more advanced features, best practices, troubleshooting, and future trends. By now, you have gained a comprehensive understanding of SAP Business One and its potential to transform your business processes.

SAP Business One is a powerful and flexible ERP solution designed to streamline operations, improve efficiency, and provide valuable insights for informed decision-making. With its extensive functionalities and integration capabilities, it enables businesses of all sizes to manage their operations effectively.

As you continue your journey with SAP Business One, here are some key takeaways and final thoughts to keep in mind:

Business Alignment: Ensure that your implementation and usage of SAP Business One align with your business objectives and processes. Continuously evaluate and adjust the system to meet evolving business needs.

Training and User Adoption: Invest in comprehensive user training to empower your team to leverage the full potential of SAP Business One. Encourage user engagement, collaboration, and feedback to foster a culture of continuous improvement.

System Administration and Support: Pay attention to system administration tasks, regular maintenance, and data backups to ensure the smooth operation and security of your SAP Business One environment. Seek support through various channels, such as SAP support, user communities, and SAP partners, when facing challenges or seeking guidance.

Data-Driven Decision-Making: Leverage the reporting and analytics capabilities of SAP Business One to gain valuable insights into your business performance. Utilize advanced analytics, integration with emerging technologies, and predictive modeling to make data-driven decisions for growth and success.

Embracing Innovation: Stay updated with the latest trends and innovations in SAP Business One, such as cloud technology, AI and machine learning, IoT integration, and enhanced user experiences. Continuously explore new features and functionalities that can bring added value to your business.

Remember, SAP Business One is a robust solution, but its true potential lies in how well you utilize it to align with your unique business requirements. Regularly assess your processes, embrace continuous improvement, and leverage the resources available to you to optimize the benefits of SAP Business One.

Thank you for embarking on this learning journey with "Mastering SAP Business One." We hope this book has provided you with the knowledge and guidance needed to become proficient in SAP Business One and drive your organization's success.

Best wishes on your continued success with SAP Business One!

Printed in Great Britain
by Amazon

40281243R00056